the divine DROP STITCH™

Designs by Kara Gott Warner

HOUSE of WHITE BIRCHES

PUBLISHERS
SINCE 1947

Table of Contents

Stuyvesant Shrug,
page 13

Union Square Market Bag,
page 28

Continental Divide Cozy,
page 33

Waldorf Wrap,
page 24

Introduction

I'd like to welcome you to the world of *The Divine Drop Stitch*, where you'll find a quirky collection of boutique-quality drop stitch designs that are both brilliantly simple to make and fashion forward at the same time.

When I first learned how to work the Drop Stitch, I was immediately drawn to this technique because there's something so liberating about dropping a stitch intentionally. It's also so simple to master, and it's such a great method for adding visual interest to just about any design.

In my experience as a knitter, I haven't had much luck in finding pattern books with innovative and easy Drop Stitch approaches that offer variations on this technique. If you're new to working the Drop Stitch, you'll see that the projects within incorporate the basics, along with a mix of innovative approaches for those of you with an eye for design.

I've also chosen an inspiring selection of yarns that allow the Drop Stitch techniques to shine! I've included some worsted weight yarns that add texture and dimension, while other projects lend themselves perfectly to bulky weight yarns that accentuate the elongated look of the stitches.

Through your own exploration, you may find that this book ignites your creative energies, and unlocks the door to the endless possibilities that working the Drop Stitch offers. I hope you have as much fun knitting these projects as I had designing them.

Enjoy!

Kara

Drop Stitch Techniques

The Techniques

The following techniques are the Drop Stitch Methods used throughout the book. Some are combined together in certain projects, while other designs may utilize one technique throughout. While working through the book, you'll find that the possibilites are endless for these simple-to-master techniques.

Basic Drop Stitch (DS)

Step 1: Work to the point to where the drop stitch will occur, and remove the next stitch from the needle.

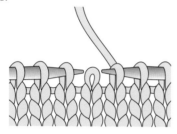

Step 2: Allow the stitch to unravel several rows.

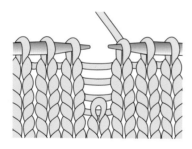

Step 3: Complete the drop stitch by allowing the stitch to unravel all the way down to the cast-on row, or to the row where the stitch originated.

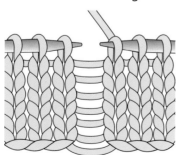

Horizontal Strand Pick-Up

This technique is the same as the Basic Drop Stitch, except that in addition to allowing the dropped stitch to unravel to the cast-on row, you pick up the horizontal section of yarn that remains after dropping the stitch. Picking up this strand maintains the original stitch whereas dropping the stitch decreases the number stitches. Examples of this technique are found in the Palladium hat and scarf, the Tassels & Triangles table runner, the Serendipity Shawl and the Stuyvesant Shrug, where the stitches are dropped and then the strands added to the stitches to replace them.

Step 1: Work same as the Basic Drop Stitch Step 1.

Step 2: Pick up the horizontal strand of yarn that remains and place it on the right hand needle to replace the stitch just dropped.

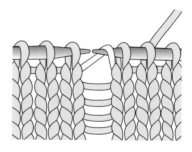

Yarn Over Drop Stitch

Step 1: Knit one stitch, then yarn over twice as shown with the lighter-colored yarn.

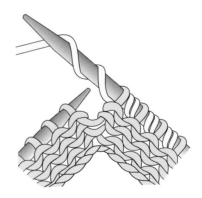

Step 2: Work across row, dropping yarn overs to create an elongated stitch as shown with the lighter-colored yarn in the illustration below.

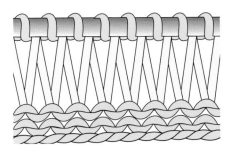

Cluster Drop Stitch (CDS)

Step 1: Drop the stitch and allow it to unravel 4 rows only.

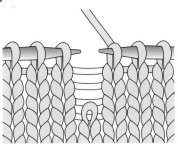

Step 2: Insert right-hand needle into stitch 5 rows below and bring needle up behind the 4 horizontal "bars" as shown with the lighter-colored yarn in the illustration below.

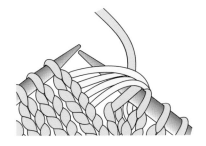

Step 3: Draw working yarn through and under 4 horizontal bars, and then back through, creating a new stitch. Place new stitch onto right-hand needle. ❖

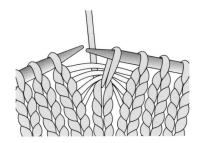

Palladium

Brilliantly simple drop-stitch effects paired up with size 3 and 15 needles create a dramatic undulating effect.

Skill Level
■■□□ EASY

Finished Sizes
Scarf: 7 x 72 inches
Hat: 21-inch circumference

Materials
- Knit One Crochet Too Linus (worsted weight; 47% wool/30% acrylic/ 23% alpaca; 98 yds/50g per skein): Scarf: 2 skeins cherry #257; Hat: 1 skein cherry #257
- Size 3 (3.25mm) straight needles
- Size 15 (10mm) straight needles or size needed to obtain gauge
- Size G/6 (4mm) crochet hook

Gauge
13 sts and 10 rows = 4 inches/10cm in garter st, on larger needle.
To save time, take time to check gauge.

Special Abbreviation
Drop St (DS): Drop st from needle, and allow it to unravel to where it originated.

Pattern Notes
Hat is made in 3 separate panels. Panels are joined together using a single crochet.

Refer to Drop Stitch Techniques on page 4 for information on working the Drop Stitch and Horizontal Strand Pick-Up.

Scarf
With larger needles, cast on 20 sts.

Beg on RS, *work in St st for 6 rows; change to size 3 needle and work in St st for 12 rows; rep from * until scarf measures approx 71 inches.

Next row (Drop St row): K2, DS, pick up horizontal strand of yarn that remains and place on the RH needle to replace the st, k14, DS, pick up horizontal strand of yarn that remains and place on the RH needle to replace the st, k2.

Knit 1 row.

Bind off all 20 sts.

Hat
Hat Sections
Make 3

With smaller needles, cast on 24 sts.

Knit 2 rows, purl 1 row.

Beg with RS, work in St st for 12 rows, then change to larger needles, and work 6 rows in St st. Change to smaller needles and work 2 rows St st.

Dec Row: With smaller needle, k8, [k2tog] 4 times, k8—20 sts.

Work 5 rows in St st.

Dec Row: K6, [k2tog] 4 times, k6—16 sts.

Work 3 rows in St st, ending with a WS.

Change to larger needles, and work even for 6 rows.

Change to smaller needles, and work 2 rows in St st.

Dec Row: K4, [k2tog] 4 times, k4—12 sts.

Work 5 rows in St st.

Dec Row: K4, [k2tog] twice, k4—10 sts.

Next row (Drop St row): With smaller needles, k3, DS, k2, DS, k3—8 sts.

Work 1 row even.

Next row: [K2tog] 4 times—4 sts.

Next row: [P2tog] twice—2 sts.

Next row: K2tog. Fasten off.

Join Panels
Hold 2 panels with WS tog. With crochet hook, join yarn and work row of sc from hat band edge to crown.

Hold 3rd panel with WS tog with side of panels just worked, and work a row of sc from crown to lower edge of hat. Cut yarn. Close final seam, by re-joining yarn, and working a row of sc from hat band to crown. Fasten off.

Finishing
Weave in all ends, block lightly to finished measurements. ❖

The Divine Drop Stitch

Serendipity Shawl

Turn some heads and add some glamour to your look this evening wearing this shawl with alluring linear accents.

Skill Level
 ◼◼◻◻ EASY

Finished Size
18 x 70 inches

Materials
- Knit One Crochet Too Geologee (worsted weight; 55% wool/45% acrylic; 120 yds/50g per ball): 6 balls tourmaline #583
- Size 7 (4.5mm) needles or size needed to obtain gauge
- Size G/6 (4mm) crochet hook

Gauge
18 sts and 30 rows = 4 inches/10cm in garter st.
To save time, take time to check gauge.

Special Abbreviation
Drop St (DS): Drop st from needle, and allow it to unravel to where it originated.

Pattern Notes
Shawl is made by working 30 triangles, then single crocheting them together as shown in the diagram.

Refer to Drop Stitch Techniques on page 4 for more information on working the Drop Stitch and Horizontal Strand Pick-Up.

Shawl
Triangle
Make 30

Cast on 2 sts.

Row 1: Yo, knit across—3 sts.

Row 2: Yo, knit across all sts.

Rep Row 2 until there are 35 sts on needle.

House of White Birches, Berne, Indiana 46711

Next row (Drop St row): K13, [DS, pick up horizontal strand of yarn that remains and place on the RH needle to replace the st, knit 3] twice, DS, pick up horizontal strand of yarn that remains and place on the RH needle to replace the st, k13.

Bind off all sts.

Assembly
Referring to assembly diagram on page 12, arrange all 30 triangles. Sc triangles tog.

Finishing
Weave in all ends, block lightly to finished measurements. ❖

House of White Birches, Berne, Indiana 46711   AnniesAttic.com

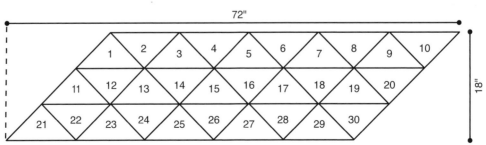

Assembly Diagram

72"

18"

1 2 3 4 5 6 7 8 9 10

11 12 13 14 15 16 17 18 19 20

21 22 23 24 25 26 27 28 29 30

Stuyvesant Shrug

This ethereal and elegant shrug showcases the basic ladder drop stitch, along with simple stockinette and garter stitching.

Skill Level

 EASY

Sizes

Woman's small (medium, large) Instructions are given for smallest size, with larger sizes in parentheses. When only 1 number is given, it applies to all sizes.

Finished Measurements

Back (across back): 16 (17½, 18½) inches
Sleeve length: 15½ (16½, 18) inches

Materials

- Rowan Alpaca Cotton (worsted weight; 72% alpaca/28% cotton; 148 yds/50g per ball): 3 balls rice #400
- Size 7 (4.5mm) straight and 24-inch circular needles or size needed to obtain gauge
- Size 10 (6mm) 24-inch circular needle

4 MEDIUM

Gauge

16 sts and 26 rows = 4 inches/10cm in St st.
13 sts and 26 rows = 4 inches/10cm in Drop St pat.
To save time, take time to check gauge.

Special Abbreviation

Drop St (DS): Drop st from needle, and allow it to unravel to where it originated.

Pattern Notes

Refer to Drop Stitch Techniques on page 4 for information on working the Drop Stitch and Horizontal Yarn Pick-Up.

Sleeves are worked as 1 piece from cuff to cuff.

Sleeves

With smaller needles, cast on 37 (37, 42) sts.

Work in St st until piece measures 35 (38½, 42½) inches, ending with a WS row.

Next row (Drop St row): K3, DS, pick up horizontal strand of yarn that remains and place on the RH needle to replace the st, *k4, DS, pick up horizontal strand of yarn that remains and place on the RH needle to replace the st; rep from * to last 3 sts, k3 sts.

Bind off all sts.

Cuff

Make 2

With smaller needles, cast on 47 sts and work in St st until cuff measures 4 inches, ending with a WS row.

Next row (Drop St row): K3, DS, *k4, DS; rep from * to last 3 sts, k3 sts—37 sts.

Work in garter st until cuff measures 6 inches from cast-on edge.

Bind off all sts.

Sew 1 cuff to each end of sleeve piece.

Assembly

Fold sleeve piece in half lengthwise. Form sleeves by sewing 15½ (16½, 18) inches from each cuff to center, leaving center section open for body.

Body

With smaller circular needle and beg at one sleeve seam, pick up and knit 105 (115, 120) sts around open center section of sleeves, place marker and join to work in rnds.

Work in St st (knit every rnd) until body measures 5 inches.

Change to larger circular needle and work in garter st (purl 1 rnd, knit 1 rnd) until body measures 8½ inches.

Next rnd (Drop St rnd): *K4, DS; rep from * around.

Bind off all sts very loosely.

Finishing

Weave in ends, block very lightly to finished measurements. ❖

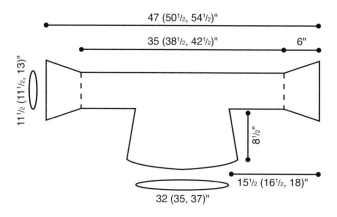

Loops & Ladders Skullcap

Featuring ladder drop stitches, this light and airy skullcap will stand out in the crowd.

Skill Level

 EASY

Size
One size fits most

Finished Measurements
Circumference: Approx 21 inches
Height: Approx 7 inches

Materials
- Rowan Alpaca Cotton (worsted weight; 72% alpaca/28% cotton; 148 yds/50g per ball): 1 ball walnut #402
- Size 7 (4.5mm) 16-inch circular and set of 4 double-point needles
- Stitch marker

Gauge
16 sts and 26 rows = 4 inches/10cm in St st.
13 sts and 26 rows = 4 inches/10 cm in Drop St pat.
To save time, take time to check gauge.

Special Abbreviation
Drop St (Drop St): Drop st from needle, and allow it to unravel to cast-on edge.

Pattern Note
Refer to Drop Stitch Techniques on page 4 for more information on working Drop Stitch.

Skullcap
Cast on 68 sts, place marker and join without twisting.

Knit 4 rnds.

Work 10 rnds in garter stitch (purl one rnd, knit one rnd).

Work in St st (knit every rnd) until cap measures 6 inches.

Next rnd (DS rnd): *K3, DS; rep from * around—51 sts.

Crown shaping
Note: Change to double-point needles when sts no longer fit comfortably on circular needle.

Rnd 1: [K2tog] around to last st, k1—26 sts.

Rnd 2: [K2tog] around—13 sts.

Rnd 3: [K2tog] 6 times, k1—7 sts.

Rnd 4: [K2tog] 3 times, k1—4 sts.

Rnd 5: [K2tog] twice—2 sts.

Bind off last 2 sts. Weave end through sts to close opening.

Finishing
Block lightly to finished measurements. ❖

Fringe Benefits

This ultra-funky duo is sure to impress with beaded fringe accents and unique Cluster Drop Stitch details.

Skill Level

■■□□ EASY

Finished Sizes

Neck Cuff: 9½ inches x 28 inches
Tote: 14 inches wide x 14 inches deep

Materials

- Blue Sky Alpaca Worsted Hand Dyes (heavy worsted weight; 50% alpaca/ 50% merino; 100 yds/100g per skein): Neck cuff: 2 skeins each mulberry #2024 (A) and charcoal #2025 (B); Tote: 3 skeins each mulberry #2024 (A) and charcoal #2025 (B)
- Size 13 (9mm) straight and 32-inch circular needles or size needed to obtain gauge
- 24 wood beads, or beads of choice with wide opening
- 1 (2- or 2½-inch) button

4 MEDIUM

Gauge

8 sts and 18 rows = 4 inches/10cm in Drop St pat with A and B held together.
To save time, take time to check gauge.

Special Abbreviations

Cluster Drop Stitch (CDS): Drop st from needle, and allow it to unravel 4 rows. Insert RH needle in st on 5th row below and bring needle up behind the 4 horizontal bars, drawing working yarn through and under the bars, and then back through st. Slip st onto RH needle.

Slide Bead (SB): Slide bead up to needle.

Special Technique

Cable Cast-On: *Place RH needle between last 2 sts on LH needle, draw yarn between sts, and place new st created in front of these 2 sts on LH needle. Rep from * for desired number of sts.

Pattern Note

Refer to Drop Stitch Techniques on page 4 for more information on working Cluster Drop Stitch.

Neck Cuff

Fringe

String 10 beads onto A and slide down on yarn and out of the way until needed.

Cast on 10 sts.

Row 1: SB up close to RH needle, and knit bead with first st.

Row 2: Bind off all but the last st. Slip last bound-off st onto to LH needle—2 sts and 1 fringe made.

Using cable cast-on, *cast on 10 sts, SB, bind off 8 sts; slip last st on RH to the LH needle; rep from * until 10 fringes are made, and 20 sts are on needle.

Neck Cuff

Join B and work with A and B held tog for rest of scarf.

Row 1 (RS): K4, [p4, k4] twice.

Row 2: P4, [k4, p4] twice.

Rows 3 and 4: Rep Rows 1 and 2.

Row 5: Rep Row 1.

Row 6 (Cluster Drop St row): P2, CDS, p1, k1, CDS, k2, CDS, p2, CDS, k2, CDS, k1, p1, CDS, p2.

Rep Rows 1–6 until scarf is 34 inches long.

Bind off loosely.

Finishing

With WS tog, fold bound-off edge up 6 inches and sew in place to form cuff opening.

Weave in ends, block lightly to finished measurements.

Tote

Fringe

String all 14 beads onto A and slide down on yarn and out of the way until needed.

Cast on 10 sts.

Row 1: SB up close to RH needle, and knit bead with first st.

Row 2: Bind off all but the last st. Slip last bound-off st onto to LH needle—2 sts and 1 fringe made.

*Cable cast-on 10 new sts, SB, bind off 8 sts, slip last st on RH to the LH needle; rep from * until 28 sts rem and 14 fringes are made.

Back & Flap

Join B and work 1 strand each A and B held tog for rest of bag.

Knit 2 rows.

Set-up pat

Row 1 (RS): K4, [p4, k4] 3 times.

Row 2: P4, [k4, p4] 3 times.

Rows 3 and 4: Rep Rows 1 and 2.

Row 5: Rep Row 1.

Row 6 (Drop St row): P2, CDS, p1, k1, CDS, k2, CDS, p2, CDS, k4, CDS, p2, CDS, k2, CDS, k1, p1, CDS, p2.

Rep Rows 1–6 until panel measures 20 inches from cast-on edge.

Bind off all sts.

Front

With A and B held tog, cast on 28 sts.

Knit 2 rows.

Work Rows 1–6 of Cluster Drop Stitch pat as for back until front is 14 inches long. Bind off all sts.

Strap

With circular needle and A and B held tog, cast on 118 sts.

Work in Garter st until strap measures 2½ inches from cast-on edge. Bind off all sts.

I-cord button loop

With A, cast on 3 sts. *Slip sts back to LH needle, pull yarn across back, k3; rep from * until I-cord measures 2½ inches. Slip sts back to LH needle and bind off all sts.

Finishing

Sew back and front pieces tog along cast-on edge. Sew each end of strap to each bottom seam. Sew cast-on and bound-off edges of strap to back and front, leaving flap at top of back unattached.

Sew I-cord button loop to center of flap. Sew button to front below button loop.

Weave in ends, block lightly to finished measurements. ❖

Breakfast at Tiffany's

These pretty mitts, worked back and forth, add excitement with central oval drop stitch styling.

Skill Level
■■□□ EASY

Size
One size fits most

Materials
- Knit One Crochet Too Brae Tweed (worsted weight; 60% merino wool/20% baby llama/10% bamboo/10% Donegal; 109 yds/50g per skein): 2 skeins berry heather #261
- Size 7 (4.5mm) needles or size needed to obtain gauge
- 2 yds 1-inch-wide ribbon, (preferably with elastic or some stretch) in color of choice

Gauge
20 sts and 24 rows = 4 inches/10cm in St st.
To save time, take time to check gauge.

Pattern Notes
Mitts are worked back and forth in rows beginning at the ruffle and working to the top of mitt.

The seam is made at the side, leaving a 2-inch opening for the thumb.

Refer to Drop Stitch Techniques on page 4 for more information on working and dropping yarn over wraps.

Right Mitt

Ruffle
Cast on 72 sts and work in St st until ruffle measures 2 inches, ending with a WS row.

Next row (RS): K2tog across—36 sts.

Next row: *K2, p2; rep from * across.

Rep last row until rib measures about 1 inch, ending with a WS row.

Next row (Eyelet row): *K2, yo, k2tog; rep from * across.

Next row (WS): Purl across—36 sts.

Work in St st until mitt measures 4½ inches from cast-on edge, ending with a WS row.

Hand
Row 1 (RS): Knit across.

Row 2: Purl across.

Row 3: Knit across.

Row 4: P21, k11, p4.

Row 5: K4, [k1, yo] 3 times, [k1, yo twice] 5 times, [k1, yo] 3 times, k21.

Row 6: P21, k11 dropping all yo's, p4.

Rep [Rows 1–6] twice.

Work in St st until mitt measures 8 inches from cast-on edge.

Bind off all sts.

Left Mitt

Ruffle
Work same as for right ruffle.

Hand
Row 1 (RS): Knit across.

Row 2: Purl across.

Row 3: Knit across.

Row 4: P4, k11, p21.

Row 5: K21, [k1, yo] 3 times, [k1, yo twice] 5 times, [k1, yo] 3 times, k4.

Row 6: P4, k11 dropping all yo's, p21.

Rep [Rows 1–6] twice.

Work in St st until mitt measures 8 inches from cast-on edge.

Bind off all sts.

Finishing

Fold mitt in half, and sew seam starting from bound-off edge about 2 inches down, leave a 2-inch opening for thumb, and then sew rest of seam closed.

Beg and ending at outer edge of drop pat, (opposite side from seam), weave ribbon through eyelets and tie ends in bow.

Rep for other mitt.

Weave in all ends, block lightly to finished measurements. ❖

Waldorf Wrap

This easy wrap offers some interesting shaping effects by combining two simple drop stitch methods to create some unexpected results.

Skill Level
 EASY

Finished Size
Appox 18 x 72 inches

Materials
- Noro Iro (chunky weight; 75% wool/ 25% silk; 131 yds/100g per skein): 5 skeins #57
- Size 13 (9 mm) straight needles or size needed to obtain gauge

Gauge
9½ sts and 12 rows = 4 inches/10cm in Oblong Drop pat.
Gauge is not critical for this project.

Special Abbreviations
Drop St (DS): Drop st from needle, and allow it to unravel to row where it originated.

Make 1 (M1): Insert LH needle from front to back under horizontal strand between last st worked and next st on LH needle, k1-tbl.

Pattern Stitch
Oblong Drop (multiple of 8 sts + 4)
Row 1: Knit across.
Row 2: *[K1, yo twice] 3 times, k5; rep from * to last 4 sts, [K1, yo twice] 3 times, k1.
Row 3: Knit across, dropping all yo's.
Rows 4 and 5: Knit across.
Row 6: K4,*[k1, yo twice] 3 times, k5; rep from * across.
Row 7: Knit across, dropping all yo's.
Row 8: Knit.
Rep Rows 1–8 for pat.

Pattern Note
Refer to Drop Stitch Techniques on page 4 for more information on Drop Stitch and working and dropping yarn over wraps.

Wrap

Cast on 44 sts.

Work Rows 1–8 of Oblong Drop pat until wrap measures 14 inches.

Next Row: *K4, M1; rep from * across to last 4 sts, k4—54 sts.

Work in garter st until wrap measures 58 inches from cast-on edge.

Next row (Drop St row): *K4, DS; rep from * across to last 4 sts, k4—44 sts.

Work Rows 1–8 of Oblong Drop pat until wrap measures 72 inches from cast-on edge.

Bind off all sts.

Finishing

Weave in all ends, block lightly to finished measurements. ❖

Union Square Market Bag

Head out to your favorite green market sporting this roomy sack, worked in garter stitch, accented with rows of yarn over drop stitches.

Skill Level
◧■□□ EASY

Finished Size
14 inches wide x 14 inches deep

Materials

- Blue Sky Alpaca Worsted Hand Dyes (heavy worsted weight; 50% alpaca/ 50% merino; 100 yds/100g per skein): 4 skeins lagoon #2023
- Size 9 (5.5mm) straight needles or size needed to obtain gauge
- Size J/10 (6mm) crochet hook
- Stitch marker

Gauge
14 sts and 29 rows = 4 inches/10cm in garter st. To save time, take time to check gauge.

Special Abbreviation
Make 1 (M1): Insert LH needle from front to back under horizontal strand between last st worked and next st on LH needle, k1-tbl.

Pattern Notes
Bag is worked in 2 pieces, each starting from strap, then joined and seamed at the sides and at the top of strap.

Refer to Drop Stitch Techniques on page 4 for information on working and dropping yarn over wraps.

Side Panel
Make 2

Strap
Cast on 10 sts and work in garter st until strap measures 10 inches.

Next row: K1, M1, knit to last st, M1, K1.

Rep last row until there are 48 sts on needle.

Work even, if necessary, until strap measures 12½ inches from cast-on edge.

Body
Row 1: *K1, yo twice; rep from * to last st, end k1.

Row 2: Knit across, dropping all yo's.

Rows 3–8: Knit.

Rows 9–16: Rep Rows 1–8.

Rep Rows 1–16.

Note: Piece should measure approx 19 inches from cast-on edge.

Bottom
Set-up row: K24, place marker, k24.

Row 1: Knit to 3 sts before marker, k2tog, k1, slip marker, k1, k2tog, knit rem sts.

Row 2: Knit across.

Rep [Rows 1 and 2] 8 times—30 sts.

Rep Row 1 until 8 sts rem.

Next row: [K2tog] 4 times—4 sts.

Next row: [K2 tog] twice—2 sts rem.

Bind off last 2 sts.

Finishing
Note: The sc joining creates a decorative edge on the RS, however, panels may be sewn on WS if preferred.

Hold 2 bag panels tog, sc around panels, starting at one edge, and working around to other. Sew ends of strap tog.

Weave in all ends, block lightly to finished measurements. ❖

Times Square

Curl up on that comfy chair with this perfect size lap blanket and matching accent pillow.

Skill Level

 EASY

Finished Sizes

Blanket: 30 inches x 40 inches (not including fringe)
Pillow: 10 inches x 10 inches (not including fringe)

Materials

- Spud & Chloë Outer (super chunky weight; 65% superwash wool/ 35% organic cotton; 60 yds/100g per skein): Pillow: 2 skeins each peat #7204 (A) and sequoia #7205 (B); Blanket: 5 skeins each peat #7204 (A) and sequoia #7205 (B)
- Size 13 (9mm) straight needles or size needed to obtain gauge
- 10-inch x 10-inch pillow form

6 SUPER BULKY

Gauge

10 sts and 11 rows = 5-inch square in Drop St pat. To save time, take time to check gauge.

Special Technique

Cable Cast-On: *Place RH needle between last 2 sts on LH needle, draw yarn through sts, and place new st created in front of these 2 stitches on LH needle. Rep from * for desired number of sts.

Pattern Stitch

Drop St Square
Cast on 10 sts.
Rows 1 and 2: Knit across.
Row 3: *K1, yo twice; rep from * across to last st, end k1.
Row 4: Knit all sts, dropping yo's from previous row, and allowing them to unravel.
Rows 5 and 6: Knit across.
Rep Rows 3–6. Bind off all sts.

Pattern Note

Refer to Drop Stitch Techniques on page 4 for more information on working the Yarn Over Drop Stitch.

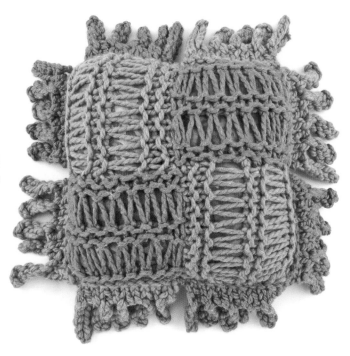

Pillow
Panel 1

With A, work Drop St Square.

Turn square. With B, pick up and knit 10 sts in ends of rows along side.

Knit 2 rows.

Work [Rows 3–6 of Drop St Square] twice.

Bind off.

Panel 2

With B, work Drop Stitch Square.

Turn square. With A, pick up and knit 10 sts in ends of rows along side.

Knit 2 rows.

Work [Rows 3–6 of Drop St Square] twice. Bind off.

Rep Panels 1 and 2 for opposite side of pillow.

Referring to Pillow diagram on page 32, join 2 panels at center for front, and 2 panels at center

for back. (**Note:** *Arrows indicate direction of knitting for each Drop St Square.*)

Fringe Section
Make 4 in A and 4 in B

Cast on 8 sts, *bind off all but last st, leaving 1 st on LH needle, and 1 st on RH needle—2 sts rem.

Slip st from RH needle to LH needle and cast on 8 sts using cable cast-on method.

Rep from * 4 times—5 fringes made.

Knit one row, bind off all sts.

Finishing
Referring to diagram, sew fringe sections around entire edge of front pillow section.

Sew back and front pillow pieces tog leaving 1 side open. Insert pillow form, and sew opening closed.

Weave in all ends, block lightly to finished measurements.

Lap Blanket

Make 12 each of Pillow Panel 1 and Pillow Panel 2. Sew Panels tog as shown in Lap Blanket assembly diagram. *(**Note:** Arrows indicate direction of knitting for each Drop St Square.)*

Make 14 fringe sections in A, and 14 in B. Referring to diagram, sew fringe sections around edge of blanket.

Weave in all ends, block lightly to finished measurements. ❖

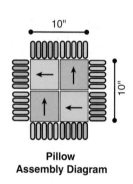

10"

10"

**Pillow
Assembly Diagram**

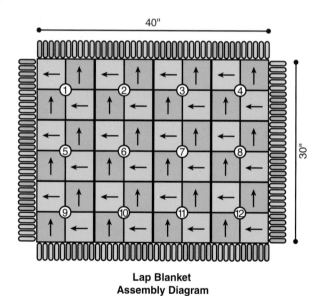

40"

30"

**Lap Blanket
Assembly Diagram**

Continental Divide Cozy

Spice up your table with this fun knit-in-the-round cozy.
Make one or two this weekend!

Skill Level
◖◼◻◻ EASY

Finished Size
Fits candle with 10- to 14-inch circumference

Materials

- Knit One Crochet Too Paint Box (worsted weight; 100% wool; 100 yds/50g per ball): 1 ball painted desert #08 (colored beads) *or* 1 ball #10 walnut plum (wooden beads)
- Size 7 (4.5mm) 12-inch circular needle or set of 4 double-point needles or size needed to obtain gauge
- 27 small round beads (or wooden beads) with holes large enough to thread through yarn
  Optional: An additional 18 small accent beads are needed to use on sides of main bead if working as shown in photo detail.
- Bead threader

Gauge
19 sts and 30 rows = 4 inches/10cm in garter st.
To save time, take time to check gauge.

Special Abbreviations
Drop St (DS): Drop st from needle, and allow it to unravel to where it originated.

Make 1 (M1): Insert LH needle from front to back under horizontal strand between last st worked and next st on LH needle, k1-tbl.

Slide Bead (SB): Slide bead up to needle.

Pattern Notes
Refer to Drop Stitch Techniques on page 4 for more information on working Drop Stitch.

Cozy can be made on either a circular needle or on double-point needles.

House of White Birches, Berne, Indiana 46711   AnniesAttic.com

Next rnd: *K2, p1, k1, p1; rep from * around.

Rep last rnd.

Next rnd (Bead rnd): *K2, p1, k1, SB up close to RH needle and knit bead(s) with next st, p1; rep from * around.

Work 3 rnds even.

Rep [last 4 rnds] twice.

Next rnd (DS rnd): *K2, p1, DS, p1; rep from * around—36 sts.

Work in k2, p2 rib until cozy measures 5½ inches from cast-on edge.

Bind off all sts.

Finishing

Weave in all ends, block lightly if desired. ❖

Cozy

Note: For cozy with wooden beads, thread all 18 beads onto yarn. For cozy with colored beads, thread 9 large beads, then 9 groups with a small, large, small sequence, then the rem 9 large beads. Push beads down on yarn and out of the way until needed. When indicated in instructions, slide beads or bead sequence up close to needle and knit with next st.

Cast on 36 sts onto circular needle *or* onto 3 double-point needles, arranging 12 sts on each needle.

Next rnd: *K2, p2; rep from * around.

Rep last rnd until rib measures 1½ inches.

Next rnd (inc rnd): *K2, p1, M1, p1; rep from * around—45 sts.

Tassels & Triangles

With eye-catching geometric shaping and crochet accents, you can set your table with style!

Skill Level
◼◼◻◻ EASY

Finished Size
14 x 84 inches

Materials
- Knit One Crochet Too 2nd Time Cotton (worsted weight; 75% cotton/25% acrylic; 180 yds/100g per skein): 3 skeins each ochre #485 (A) and berry #287 (B)
- Size 6 (4mm) straight needles or size needed to obtain gauge
- 4-inch-square piece of cardboard (to make tassels)
- Size G/6 (4mm) crochet hook

Gauge
19 sts and 30 rows = 4 inches/10cm in garter st. To save time, take time to check gauge.

Special Abbreviation
Drop St (DS): Drop st from needle, and allow it to unravel to where it originated.

Pattern Notes
Table runner is made by working 22 triangles, (11 in A, and 11 in B) then connecting them together using single crochet in your choice of colors. Tassels are made and attached on each end of the runner.

Refer to Drop Stitch Techniques on page 4 for more information on working Drop Stitch and Horizontal Strand Pick-Up.

Table Runner
Triangles
Make 11 in A and 11 in B

Cast on 2 sts.

Row 1: Yo, knit across—3 sts.

Row 2: Yo, knit across.

Rep Row 2 until there are 53 sts on the needle.

Next row (Drop St row): K18, DS, pick up horizontal strand of yarn that remains and place on the RH needle to replace the st, *k3, DS, pick up horizontal strand of yarn that remains and place on RH needle to replace the st; rep from * 3 times more, k18 sts.

Bind off all sts.

Assembly
Arrange all 22 triangles, alternating A and B as shown in assembly diagram. With either A or B sc triangles tog.

Tassels
Make 2 in A, 2 in B

With 4-inch square of cardboard, wrap yarn around cardboard approx 30 times. Cut a 15-inch length of yarn and place under all strands at one end of cardboard. Pull tog tightly and tie in knot. Cut loops at opposite end, remove cardboard.

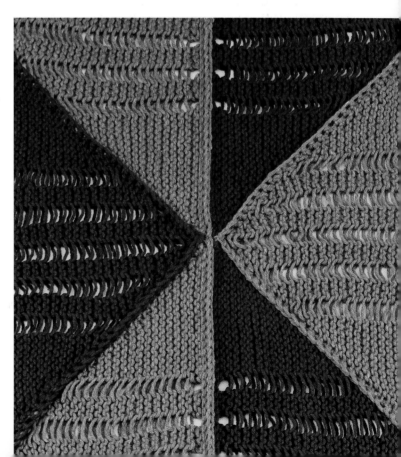

Cut another length of yarn, about 12 inches long and tie tightly around tassel about 1 inch below top knot. Wrap several times more around tassel, tie tightly into knot, and tuck threads into tassel.

Finishing

Weave in all ends, block lightly to finished measurements.

Tack tassels to ends of runner, placing A tassels on corners made in B and B tassels on corners made in A. ❖

72"

18"

Assembly Diagram

General Information

Inches Into Millimeters & Centimeters
All measurements are rounded off slightly.

inches	mm	cm	inches	cm	inches	cm	inches	cm
⅛	3	0.3	5	12.5	21	53.5	38	96.5
¼	6	0.6	5½	14	22	56.0	39	99.0
⅜	10	1.0	6	15.0	23	58.5	40	101.5
½	13	1.3	7	18.0	24	61.0	41	104.0
⅝	15	1.5	8	20.5	25	63.5	42	106.5
¾	20	2.0	9	23.0	26	66.0	43	109.0
⅞	22	2.2	10	25.5	27	68.5	44	112.0
1	25	2.5	11	28.0	28	71.0	45	114.5
1¼	32	3.2	12	30.5	29	73.5	46	117.0
1½	38	3.8	13	33.0	30	76.0	47	119.5
1¾	45	4.5	14	35.5	31	79.0	48	122.0
2	50	5.0	15	38.0	32	81.5	49	124.5
2½	65	6.5	16	40.5	33	84.0	50	127.0
3	75	7.5	17	43.0	34	86.5		
3½	90	9.0	18	46.0	35	89.0		
4	100	10.0	19	48.5	36	91.5		
4½	115	11.5	20	51.0	37	94.0		

Knitting Needle Conversion Chart

U.S.	1	2	3	4	5	6	7	8	9	10	10½	11	13	15	17	19	35	50
Continental-mm	2.25	2.75	3.25	3.5	3.75	4	4.5	5	5.5	6	6.5	8	9	10	12.75	15	19	25

Abbreviations & Symbols

[ ] work instructions within brackets as many times as directed
( ) work instructions within parentheses in the place directed
** repeat instructions following the asterisks as directed
* repeat instructions following the single asterisk as directed
" inch(es)

approx approximately
beg begin/beginning
CC contrasting color
ch chain stitch
cm centimeter(s)
cn cable needle
dec decrease/decreases/decreasing
dpn(s) double-pointed needle(s)
g gram
inc increase/increases/increasing
k knit

k2tog knit 2 stitches together
LH left hand
lp(s) loop(s)
m meter(s)
M1 make one stitch
MC main color
mm millimeter(s)
oz ounce(s)
p purl
pat(s) pattern(s)
p2tog purl 2 stitches together
psso pass slipped stitch over
p2sso pass 2 slipped stitches over
rem remain/remaining
rep repeat(s)
rev St st reverse stockinette stitch
RH right hand
rnd(s) rounds
RS right side
skp slip, knit, pass stitch over—one stitch decreased

sk2p slip 1, knit 2 together, pass slip stitch over the knit 2 together—2 stitches have been decreased
sl slip
sl 1k slip 1 knitwise
sl 1p slip 1 purlwise
sl st slip stitch(es)
ssk slip, slip, knit these 2 stitches together—a decrease
st(s) stitch(es)
St st stockinette stitch/stocking stitch
tbl through back loop(s)
tog together
WS wrong side
wyib with yarn in back
wyif with yarn in front
yd(s) yard(s)
yfwd yarn forward
yo yarn over

Standard Yarn Weight System

Categories of yarn, gauge ranges, and recommended needle sizes

Yarn Weight Symbol & Category Names	1 SUPER FINE	2 FINE	3 LIGHT	4 MEDIUM	5 BULKY	6 SUPER BULKY
Type of Yarns in Category	Sock, Fingering, Baby	Sport, Baby	DK, Light Worsted	Worsted, Afghan, Aran	Chunky, Craft, Rug	Bulky, Roving
Knit Gauge Range* in Stockinette Stitch to 4 inches	27–32 sts	23–26 sts	21–24 sts	16–20 sts	12–15 sts	6–11 sts
Recommended Needle in Metric Size Range	2.25–3.25mm	3.25–3.75mm	3.75–4.5mm	4.5–5.5mm	5.5–8mm	8mm and larger
Recommended Needle U.S. Size Range	1 to 3	3 to 5	5 to 7	7 to 9	9 to 11	11 and larger

* GUIDELINES ONLY: The above reflect the most commonly used gauges and needle sizes for specific yarn categories.

Glossary

bind off—used to finish an edge

cast on—process of making foundation stitches used in knitting

decrease—means of reducing the number of stitches in a row

increase—means of adding to the number of stitches in a row

intarsia—method of knitting a multicolored pattern into the fabric

knitwise—insert needle into stitch as if to knit

long tail cast on—method of cast-on where length of yarn about an inch long for each stitch is left at end before making first cast-on stitch

make 1—method of increasing using the strand between the last stitch worked and the next stitch

place marker—placing a purchased marker or loop of contrasting yarn onto the needle for ease in working a pattern repeat

purlwise—insert needle into stitch as if to purl

right side—side of garment or piece that will be seen when worn

selvage stitch—edge stitch used to make seaming easier

slip, slip, knit—method of decreasing by moving stitches from left needle to right needle and working them together

slip stitch—an unworked stitch slipped from left needle to right needle, usually as if to purl

work even—continue to work in the pattern as established without working any increases or decreases

work in pattern as established—continue to work following the pattern stitch as it has been set up or established on the needle, working any increases or decreases in such a way that the established pattern remains the same

yarn over—method of increasing by wrapping the yarn over the right needle without working a stitch

How to Check Gauge

A correct stitch gauge is very important. Please take the time to work a stitch gauge swatch about 4 x 4 inches. Measure the swatch. If the number of stitches and rows are fewer than indicated under "Gauge" in the pattern, your needles are too large.

Try another swatch with smaller-size needles. If the number of stitches and rows are more than indicated under "Gauge" in the pattern, your needles are too small. Try another swatch with larger-size needles.

Skill Levels

BEGINNER

EASY

INTERMEDIATE

EXPERIENCED

Beginner projects for first-time knitters using basic stitches. Minimal shaping.

Easy projects using basic stitches, repetitive stitch patterns, simple color changes and simple shaping and finishing.

Intermediate projects with a variety of stitches, mid-level shaping and finishing.

Experienced projects using advanced techniques and stitches, detailed shaping and refined finishing.

3-Needle Bind-Off

Use this technique for seaming two edges together, such as when joining a shoulder seam. Hold the edge stitches on two separate needles with right sides together.

With a third needle, knit together a stitch from the front needle with one from the back.

Repeat, knitting a stitch from the front needle with one from the back needle once more.

Slip the first stitch over the second.

Repeat, knitting a front and back pair of stitches together, then bind one off.

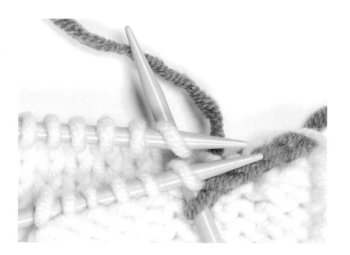

Knitting Basics

Cast-On

Leaving an end about an inch long for each stitch to be cast on, make a slip knot on the right needle.

Place the thumb and index finger of your left hand between the yarn ends with the long yarn end over your thumb, and the strand from the skein over your index finger. Close your other fingers over the strands to hold them against your palm. Spread your thumb and index fingers apart and draw the yarn into a "V."

Place the needle in front of the strand around your thumb and bring it underneath this strand. Carry the needle over and under the strand on your index finger.

Draw through loop on thumb.

Drop the loop from your thumb and draw up the strand to form a stitch on the needle.

Repeat until you have cast on the number of stitches indicated in the pattern. Remember to count the beginning slip knot as a stitch.

Cable Cast-On

This type of cast-on is used when adding stitches in the middle or at the end of a row.

Make a slip knot on the left needle. Knit a stitch in this knot and place it on the left needle. Insert the right needle between the last two stitches on the left needle. Knit a stitch and place it on the left needle. Repeat for each stitch needed.

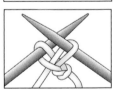

Knit (k)

Insert tip of right needle from front to back in next stitch on left needle.

Bring yarn under and over the tip of the right needle.

Pull yarn loop through the stitch with right needle point.

Slide the stitch off the left needle. The new stitch is on the right needle.

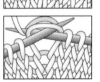

Purl (p)

With yarn in front, insert tip of right needle from back to front through next stitch on the left needle.

Bring yarn around the right needle counterclockwise. With right needle, draw yarn back through the stitch.

Slide the stitch off the left needle. The new stitch is on the right needle.

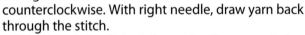

Bind-Off

Binding off (knit)

Knit first two stitches on left needle. Insert tip of left needle into first stitch worked on right needle and pull it over the second stitch and completely off the needle.

Knit the next stitch and repeat. When one stitch remains on right needle, cut yarn and draw tail through last stitch to fasten off.

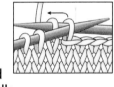

Binding off (purl)

Purl first two stitches on left needle. Insert tip of left needle into first stitch worked on right needle and pull it over the second stitch and completely off the needle.

Purl the next stitch and repeat. When one stitch remains on right needle, cut yarn and draw tail through last stitch to fasten off.

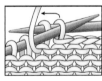

Increase (inc)

Two stitches in one stitch

Increase (knit)
Knit the next stitch in the usual manner, but don't remove the stitch from the left needle. Place right needle behind left needle and knit again into the back of the same stitch. Slip original stitch off left needle.

Increase (purl)
Purl the next stitch in the usual manner, but don't remove the stitch from the left needle. Place right needle behind left needle and purl again into the back of the same stitch. Slip original stitch off left needle.

Invisible Increase (M1)
There are several ways to make or increase one stitch.

Make 1 with Left Twist (M1L)
Insert left needle from front to back under the horizontal loop between the last stitch worked and next stitch on left needle.

With right needle, knit into the back of this loop.

To make this increase on the purl side, insert left needle in same manner and purl into the back of the loop.

Make 1 with Right Twist (M1R)
Insert left needle from back to front under the horizontal loop between the last stitch worked and next stitch on left needle.

With right needle, knit into the front of this loop.

To make this increase on the purl side, insert left needle in same manner and purl into the front of the loop.

Make 1 with Backward Loop over the right needle
With your thumb, make a loop over the right needle.

Slip the loop from your thumb onto the needle and pull to tighten.

Make 1 in top of stitch below
Insert tip of right needle into the stitch on left needle one row below.

Knit this stitch, then knit the stitch on the left needle.

Decrease (dec)

Knit 2 together (k2tog)
Put tip of right needle through next two stitches on left needle as to knit. Knit these two stitches as one.

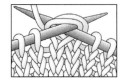

Purl 2 together (p2tog)
Put tip of right needle through next two stitches on left needle as to purl. Purl these two stitches as one.

Slip, Slip, Knit (ssk)
Slip next two stitches, one at a time, as to knit from left needle to right needle.

Insert left needle in front of both stitches and work off needle together.

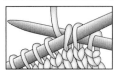

Slip, Slip, Purl (ssp)
Slip next two stitches, one at a time, as to knit from left needle to right needle. Slip these stitches back onto left needle keeping them twisted. Purl these two stitches together through back loops.

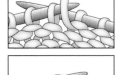

House of White Birches, Berne, Indiana 46711 AnniesAttic.com

Crochet Basics

Some knit items are finished with a crochet trim or edging. Below are some abbreviations used in crochet and a review of some basic crochet stitches.

Chain Stitch (ch)

Begin by making a slip knot on the hook. Bring the yarn over the hook from back to front and draw through the loop on the hook.

For each additional chain, bring the yarn over the hook from back to front and draw through the loop on the hook.

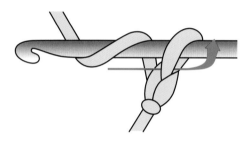

Slip Stitch (sl st)

Insert hook under both loops of the stitch, bring yarn over the hook from back to front and draw it through the stitch and the loop on the hook

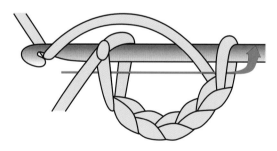

Half Double Crochet (hdc)

Yo, insert hook in st, yo, pull through st, yo, pull through all 3 lps on hook.

Single Crochet (sc)

Insert the hook in the second chain through the center of the V. Bring the yarn over the hook from back to front.

Draw the yarn through the chain stitch and onto the hook.

Again bring yarn over the hook from back to front and draw it through both loops on hook.

For additional rows of single crochet, insert the hook under both loops of the previous stitch instead of through the center of the V as when working into the chain.

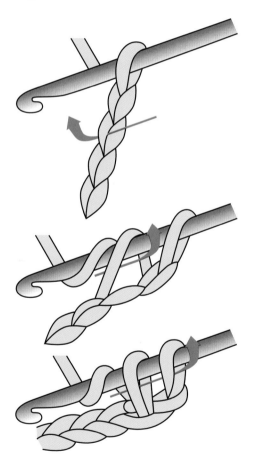

Knitting With Beads

Threading beads onto yarn is the most common way to knit with beads.

Step 1: Before beginning to knit, thread the beads onto your skein of yarn using a bead threader. As you work, unwind a small quantity of yarn, each time sliding the beads towards the ball until needed. Pass the yarn through the loop of the threader and pick up beads with the working end of the needle.

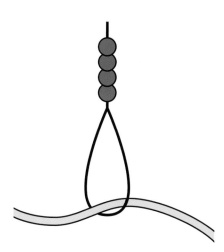

Step 2: Slide the beads over the loop and onto the yarn.

Photo Index

7

19

9

13

16

22

24

30

33

28

35

House of White Birches, Berne, Indiana 46711   AnniesAttic.com

Meet the Designer

Kara Gott Warner
It all started back in 1990-something, when a friend taught Kara how to crochet in-the-round, making accessories in every size and shape imaginable. She decided to retire her crochet hook for just awhile and move on to knitting. Kara first learned to knit as a young girl, but not until her early 20s did she come back to knitting with reckless abandon. She first used knitting as an escape from her hectic job in New York's Garment Center, when she couldn't wait to run over to her little "safe haven", The Yarn Connection, on Madison Avenue. Today, Kara spends her time working as a knitting editor and designing knitting patterns. To follow Kara on her knitting adventures, visit: www.sheknitsintheloop.blogspot.com.

The Divine Drop Stitch is published by DRG, 306 East Parr Road, Berne, IN 46711. Printed in USA. Copyright © 2010 DRG. All rights reserved. This publication may not be reproduced in part or in whole without written permission from the publisher.

RETAIL STORES: If you would like to carry this pattern book or any other DRG publications, visit DRGwholesale.com.

Every effort has been made to ensure that the instructions in this pattern book are complete and accurate. We cannot, however, take responsibility for human error, typographical mistakes or variations in individual work. Please visit AnniesCustomerCare.com to check for pattern updates.

ISBN: 978-1-59217-304-4

2 3 4 5 6 7 8 9